BE:

———

THE JOY OF SLOWING DOWN & STAYING PRESENT

PAMELA SOMMERS

Edited by Diana McMahon Collis

Print ISBN: 978-1-9163587-6-8

Epub ISBN: 978-1-9163587-7-5

DISCLAIMERS

Book

The methods described within this book are the author's personal thoughts. They are not intended to be a definitive set of instructions.

You may discover there are other methods and materials to accomplish similar results.

Although the author has made every effort to ensure that the information in this book was correct, the author does not assume and hereby disclaims any liability to any party for any loss, damage, or disruption caused by errors or omissions, whether such errors or omissions result from negligence, accident, or any other cause.

Some names and identifying details have been changed to protect the privacy of individuals.

Legal

To any person reading or following the information in this book,

references are provided for informational purposes only and do not

constitute endorsement of any websites or other sources.

Medical

Before beginning any new exercise program, it is recommended that you seek medical advice from your personal physician. This book is not intended to be a substitute for the medical advice of a licensed physician. The reader should regularly consult with their doctor in any matters relating to his or her health.

~

I dedicate this book to you,
I hope it helps you through your
journey in life,
inspires you to find
joy in the present moment,
and to have the courage to be here now.

INTRODUCTION

~

Life, fascinating as it can be, can also be pretty complicated at times. With all the roles we play, whether this is mother, wife, sister, father, husband, son, etc., it's not often that we can—well, just 'be'.

Which brings me to the reason why I wrote this book. It was Christmas time, when everybody was rushing about trying to decide on what presents to buy, what meat to eat, and frantically meeting work deadlines and the like. There I was, too, rushing around trying to please everybody—to be there to support others – whilst also having an art exhibition to prepare for.

The big day was drawing closer and then, BOOM! I had an unexpected accident which caused an injury to my back and I therefore couldn't move around easily. That was it! I felt had no choice but to lay there still, feeling sorry for myself. As time went on, the more frustrated I became. Luckily, I did have help at home from my loving family. I dread to think what it would have been like if I hadn't.

Eventually I did start to gain movement and began walking again, albeit very slowly. I was certainly learning the lesson of patience in a big way. I kept telling myself that this was happening for a reason. I wasn't sure why, but there had to be a reason for it. There I was, going about my day, and then suddenly everything had changed. The worst of all was that I had to depend on others to help me do even the smallest of things. For an independent person that was a tough pill to swallow!

Then, one day, it suddenly dawned on me; rather than 'doing' at this point in time, I had no choice but to just 'be'. That is what led me to start writing this book.

In a world where things can quickly get so complicated, why not keep it simple instead? This way we hopefully minus the stress and get to just 'be'. I say 'get to' because, if you are wise and make things simpler, not only can it make it easier on yourself, but you won't need to be charging around at a pace that's not good for your physical or mental health. There's no need for an illness or accident to take you out, since you get to a point where just *being* comes naturally to you. When it becomes that natural, you'll wish you'd started the concept sooner.

I for one wish I had done, but, hey-ho, we live, and we learn—and, boy, did I learn.

In this book, drawing from my personal life experience along with training in NLP (Neuro Linguistic Programming), Psychotherapy and Psychology, I have put together some quick pointers set out in bite-sized pieces to guide you. Please think of them as signposts, steering you to a path that helps you keep things simple, without over-whelm, so you can stress less. The best bit is that you get to just *be*.

Sound good?

Great! Let me show you the way.

1

BEING YOU

~

In a world that often encourages conformity and comparison, embracing your authentic self is a powerful act of self-expression and personal growth. Being yourself is not only important, it brings a myriad of benefits to your self-esteem, self-worth, and mental and emotional well-being, as well as overall life satisfaction.

You can allow yourself permission to be true to yourself and explore the positive impact of this on various aspects of your life, by using actionable steps to develop the confidence to embrace your uniqueness without the need for comparison.

Here are the best bits about being yourself:

- Authenticity, which lies at the core of our identity, is a reflection of our values, beliefs, passions, and desires. When we embrace who we truly are, we foster a genuine connection with ourselves and others. Numerous studies have shown that people who are authentic experience higher levels of happiness, life satisfaction, and overall psychological well-being.
- Boosts to your self-esteem and self-worth. By being true to ourselves, we cultivate a strong sense of confidence and self-acceptance. When we value our own uniqueness instead of comparing ourselves with others, we experience a significant increase in self-esteem. People who are authentic have a greater sense of

self-worth and are less likely to seek external validation.

- Embracing your authentic self has a profound impact on your daily life, enhancing your interactions. When you allow your true self to shine, you attract people and opportunities that align with your genuine interests and aspirations. By staying true to your values, you build stronger and more authentic relationships, fostering a sense of belonging and support.

Developing Confidence without Comparison

True confidence lies in recognising that we are all unique individuals with our own strengths and weaknesses; there's no need, therefore, to keep comparing yourself with others.

Having said that, it's easier said than done. So, here are some practical strategies to help you develop the confidence to be yourself:

Self-Reflection

Take time to explore your values, passions, and interests. Reflect on what makes you truly happy and align your choices accordingly.

Self-Acceptance

Embrace your imperfections and understand that they contribute to your uniqueness. Practice self-compassion and let go of unrealistic expectations.

Setting Boundaries

Clearly define your personal boundaries and communicate them assertively. This empowers you to protect your values and stay true to yourself in various situations.

Celebrating Uniqueness

Embrace your individuality and appreciate the diversity in others. Focus on personal growth and self-improvement, instead of comparing yourself with others.

Mental and Emotional Well-being

Embracing authenticity has a profound impact on our mental and emotional well-being. People who are true to themselves experience reduced levels of stress, anxiety, and depression. By aligning your actions with your core values, you create a sense of congruence and inner harmony.

Cultivating a More Balanced, and Happier Life

When we fully embrace our authentic selves, we create a more balanced and fulfilling life. By making choices that align with our true desires, we experience a deeper sense of purpose and satisfaction. Studies have shown that individuals who are authentic in their pursuits are more likely to achieve their goals and experience a greater sense of fulfilment.

It's funny how much time we spend in our heads, imagining ourselves in other people's shoes, trying on different personalities like clothes in a shop. But for now, how about taking a detour? By which I mean, talking about the most thrilling, unique, and fantastic character you could ever hope to embody, you. Yes, you heard right! So, grab a cup of your favourite beverage, sit back, and let's get started.

Firstly, we need to comprehend that being you is a journey of discovery, not a destination. Each day is an opportunity to understand more about your desires, strengths, and quirks. Now, you might ask, 'How exactly do I do that?'

Well, I'm glad you did. The answer is to start with a personal SWOT analysis. That is, identify your:

- Strengths
- Weaknesses
- Opportunities
- Threats

Embrace all of those, for they make you who you are. Write them down and keep updating the list as you grow. It'll be like a friendly, enlightening chat with yourself.

Remember, however, that acknowledging your weaknesses is not an invitation to self-deprecation. It's about knowing where you stand and what you can work on. For instance, if public speaking sends chills down your spine (believe me, I've been there, done that), take it as an opportunity to learn. Try joining a public speaking club or practicing in front of friends. Rome wasn't built in a day, and neither are our skills and confidence. So, don't be too hard on yourself.

Next up, we have this fascinating concept called self-compassion. Imagine this: your friend messed up a presentation. Would you berate them, or tell them that it's okay, that everyone makes mistakes? Now, what if YOU messed up? Often, we are our harshest critics. Try showing some compassion to yourself, instead, just like you would to a friend. Each time you stumble, pick yourself up, dust off the self-doubt and say, 'It's okay, I'm learning.'

Finally, this is the most crucial part: stop playing the comparison game. I know, easier said than done, right? But here's the thing: someone else's success doesn't determine your worth. Their life is their story, and yours is a different, equally valid narrative. A fun trick I often use is visualising myself as the protagonist of my life. Protagonists don't waste time comparing; they're too busy facing challenges, growing, and becoming the best version of themselves. So, what's your story?

Let's explore more on the SWOT analysis I mentioned earlier.

A personal SWOT analysis involves examining your Strengths, Weaknesses, Opportunities, and Threats. It's a powerful tool that can help you understand yourself better and make plans based on your capabilities and circumstances. Here's a framework for how you can do it, by observing:

Strengths

What do you excel at? This could be anything from skills you've honed over the years, innate talents, or positive qualities that others often commend you for. Are you an exceptional listener? Do you have a knack for problem-solving? It's time to give yourself some well-deserved credit.

Weaknesses

These are areas you might need to improve on. Remember, acknowledging any weaknesses is not a sign of failure but a step towards self-improvement. Perhaps you're a procrastinator, or public speaking isn't your forte. That's okay. Once you identify these areas, you can devise strategies to tackle them.

Opportunities

These are external circumstances that could benefit you. Maybe there's a workshop that can help you develop a skill, a mentor who could guide you, or a new project that would expose you to different experiences.

Threats

These are external factors that might impede your growth. This could include a competitive job market, financial constraints, or even a challenging work-life balance. Identifying these factors can help you to devise contingency plans.

Now, onto the next part; curbing the tendency to compare yourself with others. Here is a handful of practical tips:

Awareness

The first step is to catch yourself in the act of comparing. Once you're aware of what you're doing, you can consciously redirect your thoughts.

Gratitude

Spend a few moments each day focusing on what you're thankful for in your life. This positive habit shifts your attention from what others have, to what you have.

Celebrate Your Wins

No matter how small they may be, celebrate your victories. This helps reinforce the fact that you're making progress, which is what truly matters.

Limit Social Media

Social media is often a highlight reel of others' lives, leading to unfavourable comparisons. Designate specific times for social media and don't let it dominate your day.

As for being your own best friend, it essentially means treating yourself with the same kindness, respect, and support you'd give a dear friend. Here are some ways to do this:

Practice Self-Care

Dedicate time each day to do something you love – read a book, take a walk, play an instrument; anything that brings you joy and relaxation.

Positive Affirmations

Encourage yourself with positive statements, such as 'I am capable,' or 'I am learning and growing.'

Forgive Yourself

We all make mistakes. Instead of dwelling on

them, accept that they're part of being human. Learn from these, and move on.

Set Boundaries

Learn to say no when you need to. It's important to respect your own time, energy, and personal space.

Don't worry if you find this tough at first. Remember, these techniques are a journey, not a destination. Every step you take towards understanding and loving yourself more is a victory, so celebrate those steps and keep going; the rewards can be immense and definitely worth it.

These ideas are tools for your self-discovery kit, and they work best by taking consistent small steps. Remember, being yourself is not only an act of self-love but also an invitation for others to do the same. While I'll admit there can be times when this isn't easy, I believe it'll be worth every moment. Because, my friend, there's no one else like you in this vast universe. And that is your superpower!

2
———

SLOW DOWN

⁓

We live in a fast-paced world, often filled with monumental highs and deeply felt lows. It's so easy to get carried away and lost in all the crazy.

To put things into perspective, how often do you get the chance to slow down and take it easy? Not much, I'm guessing.

This is fine if you're happy living your life at a hundred miles per hour, eagerly awaiting the latest, in an effort to be the first at something. But living like that can be a constant battle, and especially so if competition is your middle name – like it was for the former version of myself. I can recall several occasions where I got a thrill simply from competing. The prize did have to motivate me enough to want to try. But then I would put everything else on hold, which meant my entire life basically, as I put all my energy into winning. Being a naturally, tunnel-visioned person, I was very driven. It was as though I saw nothing else but the end goal. And the closer I got to it, the more deter-mined I became. I also often won. I guess I just wanted it more than some of the others who competed. While that didn't win me many friends, it did mean I got noticed—and I felt I had accomplished something, however short-lived that experience may have been.

On the other hand, I would also be lying awake at night, thinking that this wasn't what life was supposed to be like; there must be more! If you've ever wondered the same, then you've hit the nail on the head, my friend, without even realising it. It's the 'more' piece that's the *real* issue.

Wanting more time, more money, more fun, more friends, more holidays, more cars… more, more, more. When will it ever be enough? The truth is it never will. It's a never-ending void that, no matter how much you have, it'll never be enough. That's because it comes from a place of not being 'enough'—correction, not feeling 'enough'. You are actually enough already; you just think you're not. This stems from a belief that has been formed in an earlier part of your life and this is perhaps why you feel guilty for slowing down and taking a break. You worry that you might miss something big; the next new thing, the latest trend or gadget. You name it, you'll imagine it, and think you're missing out.

What you may not realise is that slowing down can actually enhance your creativity, as well as your performance and general mental ability. Slowing down doesn't mean it's the end, it just means pausing, before you're ready to continue again. Slowing down is necessary, so you can gather energy and then pick up momentum once more because you've had the chance to slow down. This puts you leagues ahead of your counterparts who chose, instead, to keep going. By the time they reach near to the top of the mountain, they are running out of steam. You, however, are feeling pumped and ready to go, at just the right time. Slowing down keeps you steps ahead of your competitor and makes you stronger, physically, emotionally and mentally. Remember the story of the tortoise and the hare? Precisely.

In a world that seems to be constantly accelerating, the importance of slowing down has become increasingly evident. Slowing down is not about being lazy or unproductive; on the contrary, it's a deliberate choice to take life at a more measured and mindful pace.

Let's explore this further and start by getting to the basics. What does it mean to slow down?

To slow down doesn't mean to stop. Instead, it means to make a conscious decision to create space in your life; space that allows you to be fully present and engaged in each moment. It means embracing a more relaxed and intentional approach, rather than rushing through tasks, or constantly seeking productivity. Slowing down entails savouring the simple pleasures, finding balance, and cultivating a sense of inner peace.

There are many benefits to slowing down, including increased focus and mental clarity, reduced stress, and a positive impact on health. I don't know about you, but, after I've taken a break and allowed my mind to rest, I find it easier to think clearly. Just by taking things at a slower pace, we can lower blood pressure and help reduce other health ailments. We can also get to appreciate life and those around us more.

Applying these habits into your daily life doesn't need to be complicated either. Here are a few ideas to get you started:

Having a break

Take short, regular breaks throughout your day. During this time, check in with yourself to see how you're feeling. This has been a game changer for me. Do some simple breathing exercises, such as taking a slow inhale in for a count of three and exhaling for the count of six for a couple of times; this can help with connecting and recalibrating, without the added pressure that is so often placed upon us during daily life. It can instantly help you feel calmer and more centred, ready to continue your day.

Simplifying your schedule

Streamline your schedule to allow for adequate rest and reflection, and to evaluate any requests that are important to you. Work on prioritising them according to your values as much as you can.

Engaging in Slow Activities

Incorporate activities that naturally encourage a slower pace into your routine. Examples include:

- reading a book
- enjoying a leisurely walk, especially in nature
- practicing some gentle exercise

- indulging in hobbies that promote mindfulness, such as painting or gardening

These activities provide an opportunity to immerse yourself fully in the present moment.

Slowing down is an antidote to the overwhelming speed and demands of modern life. By consciously choosing to embrace a slower pace, we can experience numerous benefits for our mental, physical, and emotional well-being.

These include:

- improved focus
- reduced stress levels
- enhanced emotional resilience
- better physical health

In slowing down, we are enhancing our daily experiences which allows us to live more fulfilled, happier, and stress-free lives.

3

BEING STILL

~

In our constantly connected world, the art of being still has become increasingly rare. With the relentless demands of work, technology and social obligations, finding moments of stillness may seem like a luxury. It's in these moments of solitude, however, that we can discover profound benefits for our mental, physical, and emotional well-being.

Being still gives us the chance to regroup. Giving yourself the opportunity to recharge and recalibrate means you then have the courage and energy to keep going and carry on. Stillness is an opportunity to get quiet and focus our thoughts. It provides a space where we can realign ourselves and assess where we are, Like a compass it helps us to re-focus and decide on where we are going next, so we can reflect and take a new course of action if necessary.

Stillness is not merely the absence of movement; it's a state of mind and being. It's the intentional act of stepping away from the noise and distractions of life, to find inner peace and tranquility. It involves quietening the mind, calming the body, and creating space for reflection and self-awareness. Stillness allows us to be fully present in the moment and to reconnect with our inner selves.

For instance, have you ever stopped to marvel at a still lake? It's serene and tranquil, and also seems to hold a sense of depth. That's the kind of transformation we can bring into our lives when we learn to cultivate stillness. It's the wonderful art of being present in the moment, instead of fretting about the past or stressing over the future. In today's, busy world, where our attention is constantly tugged in a million directions, learning to be still can be a true game-changer.

I can recall a time when I worked in a busy school office where there were multiple things going on. Parents were dropping messages in for their children, the intercom was going off, the phones were ringing, and staff were dropping by needing help with the photocopier. My attention was in demand from numerous people. I would often take a very brief moment to gather my thoughts, helping me keep a calm approach. By doing so, I managed one thing at a time, albeit quickly, and I got all the tasks done in quantum time. It felt almost like a well-choreographed dance, with me taking one step to the left, two steps back, one hand on the phone, etc. I remember the Deputy Headteacher marvelling at my ability to remain calm during those chaotic times. Even one of the parents couldn't believe that I did it all so seamlessly—or almost. She commented, 'You know, I thought that post-it note you wrote my message on wasn't going to get done, but you did it in a flash—thank you.' I was quite new then, so the parents were still getting used to me.

The main reason behind how I managed to cope under a stressful situation like this, was that I had trained my brain and body to work together. Doing certain practices enabled me to process the things that needed to be done to create a strategy (I have always found the simple ones are the best) and take smooth action—things like:

- quiet contemplation
- meditation
- taking regular exercise
- taking a moment or two to be still and gather my thoughts

Getting into those regular habits can help when you need them most, especially during unexpected occurrences. Being still can help you manage and take control of stress. But the benefits don't end there.

Being still gives you an invaluable gift of perspective. It's like climbing to a vantage point above, and getting a bird's eye view of the landscape. You start seeing things more clearly, you understand how they connect, and, more importantly, you recognise what truly matters. By stepping back and observing, rather than getting caught up in a whirlwind of thoughts and emotions, you empower yourself. You learn to respond rather than react, to choose rather than just comply.

The practice of stillness carries a multitude of benefits, physical, mental, and emotional.

On a physical level, cultivating stillness can reduce stress. As I've touched on before, stillness activities, deep breathing exercises and spending time in nature can all help lower heart rate and blood pressure, which are each linked to stress. Reducing stress hormones, such as adrenaline and cortisol can help calm the nervous system and support the body's relaxation response, promoting emotional balance and stability. When our body isn't in a state of constant

strain and tension, it has the chance to function optimally.

This includes:

- improved digestion
- better sleep
- a stronger immune system
- increased energy levels

Mentally, being still encourages us to
become more present and focused. This
helps to move away from any negative
habitual thought patterns, such as dwelling
on past events or worrying about future
possibilities. Improved clarity, focus and
presence can boost our productivity and
creativity. It also can help sharpen problem-
solving abilities, as we're better able to see
situations clearly, and from multiple
perspectives.

Stillness can help increase self-awareness. By
quieting the external noise, we can hear our
internal dialogue more clearly. This can lead
to better understanding of our needs,
desires, values, and beliefs. In essence, it

provides the space to notice thought patterns and behaviours that may not be serving us well, thus allowing for change and growth.

Emotionally, stillness allows us to build better emotional resilience. It provides us with the ability to observe our emotions without immediately reacting to them. This gives us a chance to choose a more considered response, likely improving our relationships and interactions with others. It also encourages a sense of inner peace and contentment, as we learn to find calm within ourselves rather than seeking it externally.

The practice of being still helps us cultivate a deeper sense of connection. This might be a connection to ourselves, to others, or to the world around us. It helps us realise that we're part of a larger whole and that our actions have a wider impact. This can lead to feelings of empathy, compassion, and a desire to contribute positively to our communities.

Overall, being still provides a space for us to breathe, to heal, to reflect, and to simply be.

It serves as a refuge, a source of strength, and a wellspring of insight in our bustling lives.

But how, exactly, do we begin to incorporate this stillness into our daily lives, you may ask? Well, it's simpler than you might think. We can begin with small moments of stillness.

You don't necessarily need to set a fixed time for this. You can start simply with a few minutes here and there; then increase gradually as you become more comfortable with the practice. For instance, you could start with right after waking up, then add during lunchtime, or before going to bed.

Below are some ideas on working with stillness, to help get you going:

Pausing for breath

Pause for a minute or two during your day and just breathe. Notice the air as you inhale, and how it feels as you exhale.

Observing

Observe the world around you without the urge to analyse or judge. Just be. You could do this while sipping your morning coffee, waiting for the elevator, or even during a work break.

Whenever you're ready for more, here are further, practical ways for working with stillness:

Tracking

Begin by tracking what you do now. This gives you a better idea of the ebb and flow of your daily life, such as your routines and habits. It will give you something to work with.

For an overall framework, try out the following:

For a week, pay attention to your daily routine, trying to identify any 'in-between' moments, that are, pockets of time, moments that usually pass unnoticed as you're transitioning from one task to another. It could be the minutes while you wait for the kettle to boil, for your computer to boot up, time you spend on the bus or train, or any fleeting moments before your meals. Those are perfect opportunities for practicing stillness. Try using such moments to draw your attention inward and simply observe your breath, or become aware of your surroundings.

Digital Detox

Allocate regular periods of time throughout the day to disconnect from technology. Turn off notifications, put away your devices, and allow yourself to be fully present in the moment. Engage in activities like reading, walking, and enjoying nature without distractions.

This may surprise you, but technology can also be your ally here. For instance, many of us have smartphones that are almost always within our reach. So, why not put yours to good use for your stillness practice? You could set random alarms or reminders throughout the day, and then, whenever they go off, take a moment to practice being still. There are also plenty of mindfulness apps available that can guide you through quick and easy meditations or breathing exercises, such as *Hallow*, or the *Happy Not Perfect* app, which is one I personally use. I know *Headspace* is popular too. It's probably best to try them out and see what works for you.

Having a Dedicated Space

Having a dedicated, 'quiet' space can also be beneficial. This doesn't need to be an entire room; just a small corner where you can sit undisturbed. Make it a place where you'd love to spend time. You might want to put a comfortable chair there, a favourite plant – or anything else that evokes a sense of calm. Visiting this space regularly can create a pleasant reminder to be still, within your routine.

Meditating

Set aside a specific time each day for mindfulness meditation. Find a quiet space, sit comfortably, and focus your attention on your breath or a chosen point of focus. Even

just a few minutes of daily practice can cultivate a sense of inner stillness and presence.

Journalling

Journalling is another wonderful practice
that can be combined with your stillness
routine. After a period of quiet, jot down any
thoughts or feelings that arise. Don't censor
or judge them. This process can provide
amazing insights and deepen self-awareness,
alongside your experience of stillness.

Being Patient

Most of all, be patient and gentle with yourself. Habits take time to form. There might
be days when stillness feels particularly challenging. That's all right. Remember, it's not
about achieving a perfectly quiet mind, but
making the effort to show up for yourself
every day, despite the odds. Even the act of
attempting to be still, amidst the hustle and
bustle of life, is an achievement worth cele-
brating.

Over time, you'll find the moments of stillness extending and becoming a natural part

of your everyday life. Soon, you might even find yourself looking forward to those moments of respite in your day.

What is important is consistency. Remember, stillness is not an act but a habit; like any other habit, it takes practice and persistence to master.

Above all, please be kind to yourself. Some days, you might not feel up to it, and that's okay. Your intention to be still; this, alone, is a powerful step towards a calmer, more centred you. On those days, remind yourself that you're on a journey, not in a race.

In your quest for stillness, remember, there are no destinations, only milestones. Each moment of calm, each breath taken with mindfulness, each pause in the rush of daily life is a victory in itself. Here's a little poem I wrote about stillness:

> Being still offers us
> the calm before the storm,
> the silence between dreams,
> the space between hearts.

Don't be afraid of being still, it gives hope and helps you cherish memories that might otherwise be soon forgotten.

We often don't realise the value of a moment until it has passed.

4

SURRENDER

~

The concept of surrendering may seem counterintuitive, in this demanding world. I can understand why it might sound a bit intimidating at first. Surrender? Isn't that like giving up, a sign of defeat? Well, not really. Here's how I like to think about it, surrendering is about accepting who you are, the blessings you have and letting go of the constant need to control everything. It's giving up the illusion that we're the masters of the universe, and instead, welcoming life as it comes—simple, messy, beautiful life. It's about allowing us to explore what is, not wondering what could be.

Many of us spend our lives in a constant tug-of-war with reality. We're always striving, wanting more, and fighting against what is. The result? Stress, burnout, and feeling you're running on a never-ending treadmill. But what if there's another way?

Surrendering is, indeed, that other way. It involves loosening our grip, and allowing life to unfold naturally. It's about accepting that we're not always in control—and that's okay. It's about understanding that life is, at its core, simple. It's we who complicate it.

In reality, surrendering can be a transformative practice that brings multiple benefits to our daily lives. Here is a collection of them, together with a reminder of the benefits of practicing them:

Embracing the Present Moment

One of the primary benefits of surrender is its ability to bring us fully into the present moment. By relinquishing our attachments to past regrets and future anxieties, we free ourselves from unnecessary mental burdens. Surrendering allows us to focus our attention on what truly matters, enabling us to make the most of each experience and interaction. This heightened presence cultivates a sense of mindfulness, helping us savour the beauty and richness of life.

Promoting Mental Health

By practicing surrender, we learn to accept our circumstances, reducing feelings of dissatisfaction, frustration, and disappointment. This acceptance can greatly improve our mental health, preventing, or alleviating conditions such as depression and anxiety disorders.

Developing Resilience

Life is filled with challenges and setbacks. Surrendering does not mean giving up; instead, it equips us with the ability to navigate difficulties with grace and resilience. By surrendering to circumstances beyond our control, we can adapt and respond effectively, rather than resisting or fighting against them. This flexible mindset enables us to bounce back from adversity, learn valuable lessons, and grow stronger in the process.

Reducing Stress and Anxiety

Constantly striving for control can lead to chronic stress and anxiety. Surrendering, on the other hand, allows us to release the need for control and accept the inherent uncertainty of life. When we surrender, we acknowledge that we cannot control everything, and we let go of the tension and worry that often accompanies the pursuit of control. This newfound freedom from stress fosters a calmer state of mind, improved emotional well-being, and enhanced overall health. The act of surrendering can significantly lessen our stress and anxiety levels. By not insisting on controlling everything, we allow ourselves to accept situations as they are, reducing the constant mental chatter of worry and anxiety. This results in a more peaceful and focused mind.

Peace and Contentment

When we surrender, we release the pressure of having to control every single outcome. This leads to a profound sense of peace and contentment, as we're no longer resisting the natural flow of life. Peace of mind is priceless and can also help you sleep better at night, instead of experiencing mental turmoil as you toss and turn. Feeling content, and having a peaceful mind, is an antidote to sleep deprivation.

Improving Physical Health

Chronic stress and anxiety can have severe physical health implications, including heart disease, high blood pressure, and weakened immunity. By surrendering, and thereby reducing these stressors, we can improve our overall physical health.

Enhancing Sleep Quality

Our ability to surrender and let go of day-to-day worries also improves our sleep. We are able to fall asleep faster and enjoy more restful, high-quality sleep, which is crucial for physical health and mental clarity.

Boosting Emotional Intelligence

Surrendering helps us become more in tune with our emotions. Instead of fighting or suppressing what we feel, we acknowledge and accept our emotions. This self-awareness is a key aspect of emotional intelligence, which enhances our relationships and overall life satisfaction.

Increasing Self-Awareness

Surrender involves accepting ourselves as we are, without judgment. This helps create self-awareness and self-acceptance, essential foundations for personal growth.

Strengthening Relationships

The practice of surrendering extends beyond ourselves and has a profound impact on our relationships with others. When we let go of the need to be right or to control outcomes, we create space for understanding, empathy, and deeper connections. We allow room for authenticity, understanding, and mutual respect.

Surrendering allows us to listen attentively, appreciate diverse perspectives, and collaborate harmoniously. By creating an atmosphere of surrender in our interactions, we build stronger, more meaningful relationships that enrich our lives.

Enhancing Creativity

When we're not bound by our preconceptions and fears, our minds become a fertile ground for creativity and innovation. We're open to new ideas, experiences, and possibilities. This helps to expand our potential and may even throw in a few surprises for good measure too, which is always a welcome bonus.

Boosting Self-Esteem and Confidence

As we get better at surrendering, we cultivate a deep acceptance of ourselves, imperfections and all. This acceptance boosts our self-esteem and confidence, as we no longer hinge our worth on external circumstances but, instead, recognise our inherent value.

By learning to let go of control and embracing surrender, we can find greater peace, enhanced well-being, and a more balanced existence.

As you can see, surrendering can have a tremendously positive impact on our well-being. It's certainly worthwhile trying to incorporate these habits into your daily life.

I realise that developing ongoing, new habits can prove challenging, especially when you're busy wearing lots of 'hats', as so many of us are. So, here are some suggestions to support you along the way and help you ease into it:

Enhancing Self-Awareness

Remember to start by tracking. This will help you to see where you're at and become aware of any changes that need to be made. Begin by observing your thoughts, emotions, and behaviours. Notice areas where you tend to hold on tightly or struggle with surrender. This self-awareness will serve as a starting point for growth.

Releasing the Need for Control

Identify areas of your life where you seek control excessively. Start by relinquishing control in small, manageable situations, intentionally. As you expand your comfort zone, you will gradually develop a healthier relationship with surrender.

Acceptance

Each morning, remind yourself to accept the day as it comes. You can't control everything that happens to you, but you can control how you respond.

Practicing Letting Go

Visualise your worries, fears, and expectations as physical objects. Imagine holding them in your hands, then gently letting them go. This can be a helpful practice during moments of stress and anxiety.

Practicing Mindfulness

Incorporate mindfulness techniques into your daily routine. Engage in activities that bring you fully into the present moment, such as meditation or nature walks. I personally find that cooking a meal from scratch helps me to focus on what I'm doing, especially if the heat is turned up too high! But I also enjoy the whole experience. There's something to be said for mindful cooking, and mindful eating. These can be nurturing, nourishing and deeply fulfilling.

The following, pocket-list of practices will enhance your ability to surrender to the here and now:

Meditation

Spend a few minutes each day in silence, focusing on your breath. This practice helps you stay grounded in the present moment and encourages a mindset of surrender.

Pausing before You Respond

When you find yourself in a challenging situation, take a moment to pause and breathe instead of reacting impulsively. Consider your options, then respond in a way that aligns with your values. This will help prevent any emotional outbursts or regrettable moments; you know, those all-too-familiar, 'Perhaps, I shouldn't have said that' moments, that we are probably all guilty of at some point.

Self-Reflection

At the end of each day, reflect on moments when you felt resistance or a need to control the situation. How could you have approached those moments with a mindset of surrender? Don't worry if things don't go according to plan; it isn't something to beat yourself up over. This is a work in progress exercise. Be compassionate to yourself and move forward. Use your gained insights to guide your actions the following day.

Seeking Support

There's no shame in asking for help. We all need a helping hand now and then, if only to guide us until we get to a place where we want to be.

Surround yourself with a supportive community, or seek guidance from a mentor or therapist who can help you navigate the challenges of surrendering. Their insights and encouragement could be invaluable on your journey.

Consider incorporating some of these practices into your daily routine. This could include mindfulness exercises, meditation, journaling, or simply taking a few moments each day to breathe deeply and centre yourself. This is not a one-time act, but a lifelong practice; a journey of learning to flow with life instead of against it.

Remember, surrendering isn't about giving up or being passive—it's about embracing life as it is. It's a gentle, ongoing practice of acceptance and trust. As you walk this path, remember to be patient and kind with yourself. The journey to simplicity and surrender is a marathon, not a sprint, and every step you take is progress.

Embracing the art of surrender paves the way for a more harmonious way of being,

enabling us to live with greater joy, fulfilment, and overall well-being.

5

LETTING GO

～

I find that life is sometimes like a book. Every chapter is different, with its unique storyline, characters, and lessons. And just as you would turn the page to move on to the next chapter, it can seem hard at first and you may even feel some resistance towards doing so. But letting go is necessary at times, in order to grow. You can welcome opportunities in this way. You may also be able to live a life with greater simplicity and ease.

You might be asking yourself, 'Why is letting go so very important?' Well, have you ever noticed how holding onto past hurt, resentment, and stress can weigh you down? Like an anchor tied to your ankle, any of that may prevent you from swimming freely in the vast ocean of life. Now, think how good it would feel if you could cut free from that anchor. Imagine the relief that could bring and how liberating it would feel. That is the power of letting go.

By letting go, you are able to free yourself from experiences that hinder joy and disrupt your peace of mind. You then stand to gain so much more.

Here is a reminder of just some of the many advantages of letting go:

Unburdening the Mind

One of the primary benefits of letting go is the liberation it brings to our minds. By relinquishing control over situations that are beyond our grasp, we free ourselves from the weight of incessant worry. This mental unburdening allows us to focus on the present moment, cultivating mindfulness and enhancing our ability to engage fully in the experiences that unfold before us.

Inner Peace

Letting go helps you achieve a sense of calm and tranquility within your mind and soul. By releasing past hurts and grievances, you make room for peace and positivity.

Developing Emotional Resilience

Letting go is an essential tool for developing emotional resilience. It involves recognising that we cannot control everything that happens to us, but can control how we respond. By releasing anxiety and fear, we open ourselves to the possibility of growth, adaptability, and positive change. This newfound emotional resilience equips us to navigate life's challenges with greater ease and grace.

Enhancing Relationships

The ability to let go can have a profound impact on our relationships with others. Holding onto grudges, resentments, or unrealistic expectations can strain connections and lead to unnecessary conflicts. By releasing those negative emotions and surrendering the need for control, we create space for understanding, empathy, and forgiveness. Letting go of past hurts makes it easier for you to forgive others, and by doing so, to love more deeply. It helps improve your interactions with other people, enabling you to create healthier, deeper, more authentic connections. It enhances existing relationships and paves the way for greater love and harmony with loved ones.

Finding Freedom

Letting go frees you from past constraints. It allows you to live in the present, unburdened by previous mistakes, or anxieties about the future.

Personal Growth

When you release attachments to fixed outcomes and the need for constant control, you become open to new possibilities and opportunities. This allows you to embrace change, take risks, and step out of your comfort zone. By doing this, you are able to embark on transformative journeys of self-discovery, uncovering hidden strengths that lead you to realise your full potential. Try thinking of it like this: every time you let go, you open a door to an opportunity for new experience. You give yourself the permission to grow and evolve.

Improving Health

Holding onto stress and negative emotions can impact your health greatly. Worry and anxiety may have detrimental effects on your physical and mental health. By consciously practicing letting go, you can reduce the risk of chronic stress that often accompanies negative emotions. Managing stress can also improve your physical well-being.

Letting go is a process that takes time, patience, and practice. It's not something that happens overnight. With consistency and determination, however, it can become a powerful tool in your pursuit of a simpler, happier life.

Here are some practical ways to help make the practice of letting go a part of your lifestyle:

Being Mindful

Mindfulness is about living in the present, without judgment. By being present in the moment and observing your thoughts and emotions without judgment, you'll be able to gain clarity while you distance yourself from attachment to specific outcomes. It'll also help you develop greater self-awareness, whilst teaching you to acknowledge your feelings and thoughts without being controlled by them. Just start with five minutes of mindfulness meditation every day. As you become comfortable, aim to gradually increase the time, where you can.

Practicing Forgiveness

To forgive is to be set free, especially if you realise that the prisoner is you. Forgiving isn't saying that what happened was okay, it's about choosing your peace over your past. For instance, an exercise I like to do is to write a letter to the person who hurt you expressing your forgiveness (you don't have to send it). This is for you, not them. Try it out and notice how this process makes you feel afterwards. You may be surprised with the outcome.

Embracing Acceptance

Accept that, whatever happened, it happened. Acceptance is not about agreeing or liking what happened, but about recognising it was a part of your story. Even so, it doesn't have to be your entire book! Journal about your experiences and emotions; try concluding with an affirmation of acceptance.

Staying Positive

Stay positive and surround yourself with positivity. Stick with positive people, positive affirmations and positive environments as much as you are able to.

Using Affirmations

Use of affirmations can be a powerful tool to help instil a positive mindset. Every morning, write down three things you're grateful for, plus one positive affirmation.

Here is a list of positive affirmations you may like to try; pick the ones that resonate with you:

'Today, I abandon my old habits and take up new, more positive ones.'

'Today, I am brimming with energy and over-flowing with joy.'

'My body is healthy; my mind is brilliant; my soul is tranquil.'

'I forgive those who have harmed me in my past, and peacefully detach from them.'

'I am at peace with my past, engaged in my present, and optimistic about my future.'

'A river of compassion washes away my anger and replaces it with love.'

'My thoughts are filled with positivity and my life is plentiful with prosperity.'

'I am the architect of my life; I build its foundations and choose its contents.'

Remember, the key to making affirmations work is to embody the feelings as you say them; don't just recite them, but visualise them.

Here is a selection of further affirmations you can use, to help kick-start your day with positivity and purpose:

'With every sunrise, I am renewed and ready to take on the day with vigour and clarity.'

'I am a powerhouse of confidence; no challenge is too great for me to overcome.'

'Joy is my natural state, and today I choose happiness over worry, and peace over chaos.'

'I am in harmony, and everything I need flows to me effortlessly.'

'Today is filled with opportunity; every moment is a new chance to create the life I desire.'

'I welcome this new day with open arms, knowing it is filled with endless possibilities and opportunities for success.'

'Today, I choose to focus on what I can control, and let go of what I cannot.'

'Each challenge I face today is an opportunity for growth, learning, and further success.'

Why not have some fun creating your own affirmations? I'm a firm believer in doing what works for you, because, when you enjoy the process, you're more likely to stick with it. In this way you improve the chances of achieving your desired outcome. So, go ahead, stack the odds in your favour – and enjoy each and every moment.

Reframing Perspectives

Challenge any negative thoughts and replace them with more positive, empowering beliefs. This shift in mindset allows for greater resilience and flexibility in the face of adversity.

So, the next time a negative thought pattern emerges, try this pair of actions:

Practice Cognitive Restructuring

When a negative thought enters your mind, pause and evaluate it. Ask yourself if it's true, if it's helpful, and if there's a more positive or realistic way to view the situation.

Apply Rationale

This technique, often used in cognitive-behavioural therapy, helps you challenge and change negative thought patterns. By reframing your thoughts, you can reduce the impact of negativity and open up to a more positive outlook.

To help you out with clear examples, the table on the following page shows negative perspectives with suggested, positive reframes for common everyday situations.

EVERYDAY SITUATION	NEGATIVE PERSPECTIVE	POSITIVE PERSPECTIVE
Stuck in Traffic	"This is such a waste of time. I'm going to be late again!"	"This gives me some extra time to listen to my favourite podcast or audiobook."
Rainy Weather	"The rain ruins all my plans. This day is going to be terrible."	"The rain is nourishing the earth, and it's a perfect day to curl up with a good book."
A Project Setback	"Nothing ever works out. I'm just not good at this."	"This is a challenge, but it's an opportunity to learn and improve."
Criticism at Work	"My boss doesn't appreciate anything I do."	"Feedback is a gift. It's a chance to see how I can grow and excel."
Exercise Routine	"I hate working out. It's exhausting and I never see results."	"Exercise is a celebration of what my body can do and it's making me stronger each day."
Cooking a Meal	"Cooking is such a chore. It's easier to just order a takeaway."	"Cooking is a way to nourish my body and try new, delicious recipes."
Meeting New People	"I'm not good at socialising. I'll probably make a fool of myself."	"Meeting new people is an adventure and a chance to learn interesting things."
Paying Bills	"Money just seems to disappear. I hate this time of the month."	"Paying bills means I'm taking responsibility and have the means to support my lifestyle."
Learning a New Skill	"I'll never get this. Why bother trying?"	"Every expert was once a beginner. This is part of my growth journey."
A Busy Schedule	"I'm overwhelmed. There's too much on my plate."	"I'm in demand and have many opportunities. Time management can help me navigate this."

Table 1. Reframing the everyday

Adopting a positive perspective isn't about denying difficulties or pretending that challenges don't exist. It's about choosing to focus on aspects that can empower you, finding the silver lining, or simply reframing situations in a way that reduces stress and enhances your well-being.

Getting Active

Physical activity releases endorphins, our body's natural mood-lifters. Schedule regular physical activity into your routine. It could be anything you enjoy—Pilates, dancing, walking—just get moving!

Support Network

If you find it hard to let go, don't hesitate to seek help. You're not alone. Surround yourself with a supportive network of friends, family, or professionals who can offer guidance and encouragement on your journey of letting go. Speak to a trusted friend or family member; alternatively, consider professional help such as from a therapist or coach.

By developing the habit of releasing control, worries, and anxieties, we free ourselves from the shackles of the past and the uncertainties of the future. This can enhance our well-being, enabling us to lead a more balanced life. We open ourselves up to the beauty of the present moment through this, empowering personal growth, and nurturing deep connections with ourselves and others. Letting go doesn't mean you forget the experiences or people that have hurt you. It means you're deciding not to let those things control your happiness anymore. You're giving yourself permission to move forward and write the next chapter of your life with a lighter heart, and a clearer and calmer mind.

As you progress on your journey of a calmer and more present life, remember, it's not just about letting go, but also about holding on to what truly matters—love, peace, joy and growth—as you embrace the beauty of life.

6

BREATHE

~

Many years ago, when I worked as an Account Manager in Retail Banking, I was so busy on one particular Saturday morning that I felt I didn't have a chance to catch my breath. As a person with chronic asthma, that wasn't very good. All too often, we take breathing for granted and just expect it to be there always. I did too, until in my late twenties when I suddenly couldn't catch my breath at all. I was away for a weekend in Yorkshire, England visiting my boyfriend's brother and his girlfriend, when the incident occurred. I thought this was 'it' for me!

It seemed that, the more I tried, frantically, to catch my breath, the more I couldn't do so. It was the loneliest I had ever felt, in the cold, dark, middle of the night. Eventually I managed to somehow calm down and catch my breath.

As soon as I later returned to Essex, where I was living at the time, I saw my doctor, who diagnosed that I had suffered an asthma attack. I was in shock! I knew my mother had very mild asthma, but I had never knowingly had it. The doctor went on to say that it can be developed in later life. At that point, I felt my world had ended. I had to make what seemed like many changes. They included freezing pillows, vacuuming mattresses constantly to avoid dust mites, modifying my diet, and not going to smoky areas. I already exercised a lot, but from there on in, I also had to pay great attention to my breathing. That was when I realised how important breath was and how much I took it for granted. Others around me thought I was overreacting. But, of course, how could they know? They were not present when I almost

died, due to not being able to breathe. Whatever they thought, though, I wasn't taking
any chances, especially as I had a little boy to
look after.

It took me a while to get into the many lifestyle changes I had to make, though I realise
now how much it was worth it. Even so, at
that point, I found that just being still could
prove challenging. This applies especially if
you're busy and, like many people, have a
hundred and one things going on at any
given moment, and may be partial to wearing
several different hats. I'm sure you understand what I mean when I say that sometimes resting or taking a break for even a
moment, can feel like a lifetime away; a goal
that just can't be reached. At least not yet.
But, even if you do keep getting caught up in
your busy life, try not to overlook the simple
yet necessary act of breathing.

Breathing is an automatic function that
sustains us, but it also holds incredible
power to improve our physical, mental, and
emotional well-being. By harnessing the
potential of breathing techniques, we can

unlock a myriad of benefits and cultivate a healthier, more mindful existence. This chapter explores the numerous advantages of conscious breathing and provides practical guidance on developing a habit of breathwork, for a more balanced and fulfilling life.

The Power of Breath

Breathing is a fundamental aspect of our physiology, but is often underutilised as a tool for overall wellness. When we breathe consciously, we tap into a range of benefits that impact our mind and body positively.

Breathwork is a breathing technique that can help you release stress and tension. It is often used by people who want to perform and stay on top of their game, mentally and physically; for instance, athletes, singers, actors and high achieving entrepreneurs, as well as anyone else who wants to lead life to its fullest potential.

Here are some key advantages of incorporating breathwork into our daily routines:

Stress Reduction

Controlled breathing activates the parasympathetic nervous system, promoting relaxation and reducing stress levels. Deep, intentional breaths can calm the mind, regulate heart rate, and lower blood pressure, providing an effective antidote to the anxieties of daily life.

Enhancing Mental Clarity

Breathwork techniques, such as deep, diaphragmatic breathing increase the oxygen supply to the brain. This influx of oxygen stimulates cognitive function, enhances focus, and promotes mental clarity. By improving brain function, breathwork can boost productivity and creativity.

Emotional Regulation

Conscious breathing offers a powerful tool for managing emotions. By slowing down and deepening our breath, we can activate the body's relaxation response, which helps regulate emotions and fosters a sense of inner calm. Breathwork can also facilitate emotional processing and may be particularly beneficial for reducing anxiety and anger.

Increasing Energy and Vitality

Efficient breathing techniques can optimise oxygen intake, leading to improved energy levels and vitality. By supplying the body with adequate oxygen, breathwork enhances physical endurance, boosts immune function, and aids in detoxification processes, resulting in greater, overall well-being.

Developing Breath work Habits

Cultivating a habit of breathwork requires consistency and intentionality. Like with many things, it may not come easily at first, but, once you develop the practice and get into a routine, it will soon become second nature, or at least near enough.

Here are some practical steps to help you incorporate breathing techniques into your daily life:

Awareness of Your Breath

Start by simply becoming aware of your breath throughout the day. Take a few moments to observe your breathing patterns and notice any tension or shallowness. This awareness lays the foundation for intentional breath work.

Taking Deep Belly Breaths

Practice deep diaphragmatic breathing by inhaling deeply through your nose, allowing your belly to rise, and exhaling fully through your mouth, pulling your belly in. Repeat this process several times, gradually lengthening your inhalations and exhalations. I recall doing this particular exercise often, in preparation for singing as part of my singing class. It's also good to help you calm down in moments of high stress.

Scheduled Sessions

This may seem extreme, but setting aside dedicated time each day for breathwork practice helps to turn this practice into a routine, which is beneficial to you in the long run. Treat it as a non-negotiable appointment with yourself. Begin with shorter sessions and gradually increase the duration as you become more comfortable.

Guided Breathwork

Utilise guided breath work exercises and meditation apps to help you navigate different techniques and maintain focus. These resources provide structure and guidance, making it easier to establish a routine.

Integration into Daily Activities

Integrate breathwork into your daily activities. For example, practice deep breathing while commuting, taking breaks at work, or engaging in physical exercise. This allows breathwork to become a natural part of your daily life, making it more doable.

Breathing is vital for our survival and can also be used as a powerful tool, readily available to us at all times. By incorporating conscious breathing techniques into our daily lives, we unlock the potential for improved physical health, mental clarity, emotional regulation, and overall wellbeing.

Take heart. Developing a habit of breath work requires commitment and practice, but the transformative benefits outweigh the effort by far. Try it out for yourself and see.

7

CALM

~

F inding a sense of calmness is something increasingly sought after, especially within the chaotic world that often surrounds us. The benefits of cultivating calmness extend far beyond momentary tranquility; they encompass physical, mental, and emotional well-being.

There are many benefits to being calm, such as:

Enhanced Decision-Making Abilities

A calm mind is like a still lake, reflecting clear thoughts. When we are calm, our mental faculties sharpen, allowing us to make better decisions, solve problems efficiently, and focus more effectively. Decision-making is an integral part of life. Whether it's choosing a career path, making financial investments, or simply deciding what to cook for dinner, the choices we make shape our paths. Calmness can act like a mental sieve, filtering out the fog of emotions and stress, allowing us to see the situation with clarity and perspective. This clear-sightedness can lead to more thoughtful, informed, and ultimately, better decisions.

Deepened Relationships

Human relationships are complex and can be a source of great joy as well as immense stress. A calm state can help you communicate better because, when you're calm, you tend to communicate clearly, listen attentively, and respond with empathy. Cultivating calmness, enables us, therefore, to build stronger connections, and to resolve conflicts more harmoniously.

Maintaining calm in interactions, especially during conflicts, is like navigating a ship through stormy seas with a steady hand. It allows for constructive communication, preventing the escalation of arguments and holding a space where empathy and understanding can flourish. This equanimity can deepen bonds and build a foundation of trust and respect in relationships.

Improved Health and Longevity

Remaining calm can also help to reduce stress and anxiety, thus helping to regulate the body's cortisol levels and promote a state of relaxation. By embracing calmness, individuals experience improved emotional resilience, and reduced susceptibility to anxiety disorders.

Calmness can help improve our physical health, since the mind and body are connected. Being calm offers a profound impact to our physical well-being and research has shown that relaxation can help to lower blood pressure.

Chronic stress can also wreak havoc on the body, contributing to heart disease, hypertension, diabetes, along with a host of other ailments. Calmness can be an antidote to stress. By remaining tranquil, we keep our stress hormones in check, our heart rate steady, and our mind at ease. This not only improves our quality of life but could also add years to it.

Boosting Productivity and Creativity

The ability to maintain calmness in the face of challenges is a catalyst for productivity. When we are calm, we can approach tasks with clarity and focus, efficiently managing our time and energy.

Embracing calmness enables us to unlock our full potential and achieve greater success, over time.

Take the modern workplace, for instance. It's a breeding ground for stress, with constant deadlines and never-ending to-do lists.

However, calmness can be a secret weapon for productivity. I recall a time when I was working in a busy customer service department, just after Christmas. The place was full of customers coming to return unwanted gifts. The queue was so long that it continued around the corner! Instead of becoming flustered and panicky, I took a deep breath and focused on simply serving one person at a time. I didn't attempt to look ahead at how many more people were waiting, and I paid no attention to any grumblings. Instead, I smiled sweetly and just kept serving. In next to no time, the queue dissipated and I was left feeling calm, composed and entirely unfrazzled.

A tranquil mind is free from the clutches of panic and anxiety, making it conducive for creativity and focused work. This can enhance the quality of your work and also allows you to tackle tasks with efficiency and poise.

Enhancing Your Quality of Life

More importantly, calmness can significantly enhance your life's quality. A calm individual is like an artist who sees the beauty in everyday life, appreciating the subtle nuances that a stressed mind would overlook. Whether it's relishing a cup of coffee, enjoying a walk in the park, or cherishing time with loved ones, calmness allows you to fully immerse yourself in the present moment. In my view, this can lead to a more fulfilling life.

You may feel that this is all well and good, but life gets busy, and you struggle to fit time in to achieve a sense of calm. I agree, it does take time and practice because developing calmness is a habit. But, if we try and make the effort, it can make all the difference to our lives. Start taking small steps now and you'll soon get the hang of it.

Here are a few pointers that may help you along the way:

Engaging in Mindfulness Practices and Meditation

These are some of the most effective ways to cultivate calmness. By redirecting attention to the present moment, individuals can let go of distractions and worries, fostering a state of inner peace.

Using Deep-Breathing Techniques

Deep, intentional breathing activates the body's relaxation response and helps calm the mind. By incorporating deep breathing exercises into daily routines, we can create a sense of calmness no matter how chaotic life gets.

Taking Regular Exercise

Physical activity not only improves physical fitness but also promotes emotional well-being. For instance, engaging in activities like walking, Pilates, or running, releases endorphins, which are natural mood boosters and stress relievers. These can lead to a greater sense of calmness.

Prioritising Self-Care

Prioritising self-care is essential for cultivating calmness. Making time for activities like reading, taking baths, hobbies, being creative, or spending moments in nature, nurtures a sense of inner peace. This promotes emotional balance and tranquility.

Developing a Peaceful Space

Creating a calm environment can greatly influence our mental state. Decluttering spaces, making cosy corners, or incorporating soothing elements like plants, soft lighting, or calming scents can contribute to a serene environment that fosters calmness.

Everyday scenarios can be a focus for your mission, especially if you're feeling particularly stressed and disturbed. Sometimes it can be hard to figure out how you can apply yourself practically, in the best way.

Table 2 lists a variety of everyday situations to offer an idea of how feeling calm can be put into regular use:

BENEFIT	SCENARIO	OUTCOME
Clarity in Decision-Making	Imagine you're in a supermarket, trying to choose between twenty types of cereal.	If you're calm, amidst the chaos. You can filter out the noise and pick the cereal that actually fits your taste and budget, rather than impulsively grabbing the one with the flashiest box. Oh, and you'll probably save some money too.
Improved Relationships	Think about a heated argument with a friend or partner.	If you stay calm and tune in. You'll listen, process, and respond without letting emotions dictate your words. This often leads to healthier, more constructive conversations, and you're less likely to say something you'll regret later.
Enhanced Health and Well-being	Consider the feeling of being stuck in traffic when you're already late.	If you remain calm, it's like having an invisible shield against stress. Your heart rate stays normal, you breathe easier, and you avoid the cascade of stress hormones that would otherwise flood your system, keeping you healthier in the long run.
Increased Productivity	Think of trying to work or study with a ticking clock in the background.	If you're calm, it's like you have a volume knob for the world. You turn down the distractions and focus on the task at hand, leading to better quality work and efficiency.
Greater Enjoyment of Life	Picture yourself at a crowded concert or a busy theme park.	If you're calm, it's like you have VIP access to your own personal space. You get to soak in the music or the rides, savouring the experience, rather than getting overwhelmed by the crowds and noise.

Table 2. The benefits of feeling calm

Staying calm is not just about feeling peaceful; it's like having a personal toolkit for life, equipping you to deal with challenges more effectively and enjoy the good times more deeply.

In a world that glorifies hustle and overstimulation, calmness is a radical act! It's a quiet rebellion against the chaos of modernity. Finding a state of calmness can be a relief. If it feels out of your reach right now, don't worry. Embracing calmness is not just a one-time achievement, but a lifelong journey that unfolds with patience, practice, and self-compassion.

Developing habits that promote calmness can unlock many advantages and, as you discover the profound benefits of calmness, it becomes a total game-changer. Once you tap into this almost secret key to well-being, you'll realise that perhaps life doesn't have to be so chaotic after all.

It's also worthwhile remembering that, by embracing tranquility, you're not just improving your own life; you're setting an example for others with calmness and composure. You're showing that peace is not just an end, but a means to living a more thoughtful, healthy, and joyful life.

So the next time life's tumultuous waves threaten to overwhelm you, remember the serene superpower within you, and let calmness be your guide.

8

REST

~

If there is one thing in life that is underrated and doesn't get the credit it deserves, it is rest.

Life can often be very demanding, with the feeling of being pushed from pillar to post. I'm sure you're familiar with this particular feeling, when, the moment you sit down, you're being called to do something or other and your one (or two) minute break gets disturbed. The concept of rest often takes a back seat as we strive to accomplish more, to do more, and be more. The importance of rest cannot be overstated, however. Rest is not merely a nice-to-have component, or an indulgence; it is a fundamental necessity for our overall well-being.

We often undervalue the art of doing nothing at all. Here's the insider secret that we keep missing—rest is not the antagonist to productivity; rather, it's an essential ally. Think of it as renewable energy for your mind and body. The practice of recharging and raising your battery levels from time to time gives you the ability to bounce back, feeling refreshed and revitalised. This is the extraordinary element that will keep you feeling far from ordinary. Rest may, in fact, sound simple, but it's an essential ingredient to keep you performing at your utmost best and help you realise your potential.

Although, there is more to rest then meets the eye. Contrary to popular belief—or what society likes to insinuate—rest is not for the weak; neither is it for someone who has nothing better to do with their time. Let me share something with you that I wish someone had shared with me years ago. Rest is not merely a passive state of doing nothing; it's an active engagement in rejuvenation.

Each moment you commit to rest is an investment in the health of your body, mind, and soul.

By ignoring rest, we are denying ourselves a crucial ingredient for peak performance. You see, the greatest minds throughout history were not just workaholics, they were also champions of rest. For instance, Winston Churchill was an advocate of napping and regularly took afternoon naps to help revive his energy.

Rest is the surprising secret of many high performers (Stulberg & Magness, 2017). But it has to be the right quality of rest, one that enriches your life. For instance, let's suppose you're trying to find a solution for a problem such as a work issue. Try taking time out for a walk or doing something completely different. It might be walking in nature, or sitting in the garden, for example. You may often find that, after taking that short break—indeed maybe while you're out walking—a solution comes to you; and it wouldn't have done if you'd just continued to keep your head down on the task in hand.

This kind of change occurs because the part of your brain that solves problems has been given the space to think up ideas. Have you ever tried asking a question before you fall asleep and find you wake up with the answer? The reason is, just like a computer, your brain is programmed to try to find the answer to the question; it attempts to fill in the gap, determined to complete the loop. This is why asking 'open' questions can be so fruitful.

Rest is a multifaceted concept that extends beyond sleep and relaxation. It encompasses a deliberate and conscious choice to disengage from daily routines and responsibilities, allowing the mind and body to recharge, rejuvenate and rebuild. Rest can take many forms, including sleep, leisure activities, mindfulness exercises, meditation—even just brief moments of solitude.

As we delve deeper into the world of rest, it's vital to not trivialise its immense benefits. By incorporating rest into our daily routine, we're investing in a healthier, happier, and more productive lifestyle.

Let's explore the dividends of downtime, knowing that understanding these benefits can further motivate us to prioritise rest.

Enhancing Productivity

Rest leads to enhanced productivity. It may sound counterintuitive, given our society's tendency to equate constant activity with effectiveness, but taking time for rest can actually make work hours more fruitful. Rest allows the brain to replenish its stores of attention and motivation, promotes creativity, and aids in problem-solving. It's like hitting the refresh button on your brain's browser—everything runs smoother and faster, post-refresh.

By allowing ourselves time for rejuvenation, instead of working to the maximum capacity, we can keep burnout at bay. We can also maintain motivation and enhance our overall efficiency when we return to work or other activities.

Improving Physical Health

Rest is a crucial component of physical health. Adequate rest is needed for muscle repair, memory consolidation, and the release of hormones that regulate growth and appetite. Furthermore, active rest, can, like stretching, aid in improving circulation, reducing muscle stiffness, and lowering the risk of injuries. Regular rest periods and sufficient sleep contribute to:

- better immune function
- reduced risk of chronic illnesses
- increased longevity

Greater Emotional Health

Benefits of rest also extend into the area of emotional health. Proper rest can improve mood, reduce anxiety and stress levels, and increase one's overall sense of well-being. It provides the emotional bandwidth to connect deeply with others, enjoy single moments more fully, and therefore handle ups and downs of life with greater resilience. It's like a soothing balm for your emotional health, easing the rough edges and amplifying the positives. Overall, it brings enhanced emotional well-being. Rest provides us with the opportunity to process and regulate our emotions effectively. By taking time to relax and engage in activities that bring us joy, we can reduce stress levels, combat anxiety and depression, and improve our emotional resilience.

Better Mental Clarity and Focus

Rest also offers enhanced mental clarity and focus. A well-rested mind is sharper, quicker, and more alert. It's better at concentration, memory retention, and decision-making. Adequate rest improves cognitive functions, such as attention span, problem-solving abilities, and creativity. By giving our brains a break, we allow them to consolidate information, make connections, and generate innovative ideas. When we commit to regular rest, we're also committing to a more vibrant, engaged, and effective mental state.

Deeper Connection

Rest helps us to develop a deeper connection with ourselves. In the quiet moments of rest, we find the space to reflect, introspect, and truly listen to what our mind, body, and soul are saying. Have you ever noticed that it's often while you are at leisure or resting that you find your deepest insights, your boldest ideas, and your most profound self-under-standing? Sometimes, those moments can turn out to be the most inspired. I have certainly found this, as there have been many occasions when I would wake at 3 a.m. with ideas that I simply must write down in case I forget them. These nocturnal down-loads often save me lots of daylight time and turn out to be my best work, with seemingly minimum effort—apart from the editing, of course.

So, now you have seen some of the benefits to having rest, you may be wondering, "But Pamela, how on earth can I incorporate rest into my already jam-packed schedule?"

I suggest you begin by viewing rest as an appointment with yourself, one that you can't afford to postpone or miss altogether. Set aside a few moments each day for mindful relaxation, whether that's a 15-minute nap, a leisurely walk in the park, or a peaceful meditation session. Just as you would set a meeting or a doctor's appointment, schedule a time for rest. Remember, this isn't wasted time; it's time spent refuelling your internal engine, so you can run at peak efficiency.

If you're still worried, however, about how you're going to fit this practically into your daily schedule, I have a few ideas for you:

Prioritising Quality Sleep

Aim for 7-9 hours of sleep each night, uninterrupted if possible. Create a relaxing bedtime routine, limiting screen time before bed, and ensuring your sleeping environment is conducive to rest.

Practicing Mindfulness and Meditation

Engage in mindfulness exercises or meditation to cultivate a sense of calm and reduce stress levels. Even just a few minutes of deep breathing, or guided meditation, can provide significant benefits.

Embracing Leisure and Hobbies

Set aside time for activities that bring you joy and fulfilment, whether they be things like reading, painting, gardening, or simply spending time in nature. Those moments of leisure can allow your mind to recharge and help maintain a healthy work-life balance.

The How-To Practicalities of Embracing Rest

Incorporating rest into your daily routine doesn't require grandiose gestures or significant upheaval of your schedule. It's about weaving in small, yet impactful moments of tranquility.

So, let's delve deeper into practical tips for introducing different types of rest into your life.

One of the most straightforward methods is the adoption of a daily 'quiet time'. This can be time set aside where you consciously unplug from digital devices and spend moments in quiet contemplation, meditation, or simply being present. You'd be surprised by the wonders that going screen-free can do to your mental clarity and overall stress levels. Whether it's straight after you wake or the last hour before you sleep, a 'quiet time' can become a sanctuary of serenity in your day. I do this as part of my evening routine, and it helps me drift off to sleep tremendously well.

Forms of Rest

Perhaps you've never considered this before, but there are different forms of rest. Let's explore examples of some variations:

Physical Rest

Physical rest is important and goes beyond a good night's sleep. The inclusion of short, regular breaks throughout your workday can help alleviate physical tension as well as mental fatigue, for example. Then there is 'active rest', which could be a gentle exercise session or a leisurely stroll in your neighbourhood. These kinds of activities allow your body to unwind without falling into stagnation.

You may like to try the popular Pomodoro Technique, developed in the 1980s by Francesco Cirillo (Cirillo, 1981). It's a time management method consisting of 25 minutes of focused work followed by a 5-minute break. After this has been repeated approximately four times, you can take a longer break for about 20-30 minutes and start over, if you wish to do so. This technique helps to ensure you're not straining yourself continuously. I find it especially helpful when I have a large project to work on.

Emotional Rest

Emotional rest, while is often overlooked, is just as critical. It involves allowing yourself to feel without judgment, expressing emotions honestly, and saying no when you need to. Setting boundaries isn't selfish; sometimes it's necessary. After all, you need self-care too.

Techniques like journaling can also provide a safe space for emotional rest, helping you unravel your feelings and thoughts, offering clarity and catharsis. Reflection can be an eyeopener, as self-awareness is one of the first steps of self-development.

Sensory Rest

Another, lesser-known but effective, type of rest is sensory rest. In our modern world, our senses are constantly bombarded by noises, artificial lights and screens. Engaging in activities like listening to soothing music, dimming lights, using eye masks, or earplugs can help reduce sensory overload. Sensory rest allows our often-overstimulated senses to reset and recharge.

Creative Rest

Creative rest involves engaging in activities that reignite your sense of wonder and inspire awe. This could be anything from visiting an art gallery, spending time in nature, or simply gazing at the stars in your backyard. It's about reconnecting with the world in a profound, appreciative way, stimulating the creative parts of your brain.

Remember, there's no 'one-size-fits-all' approach to rest. It's a deeply personal journey, and the types of rest you need can vary based on your current physical, emotional, and mental states. Start by acknowledging the importance of rest; listen to your body's cues, and allow yourself the grace and permission to pause, refuel, and rejuvenate. By embracing these various forms of rest, you're not only investing in yourself but also enriching the quality of your everyday life.

One of the beautiful aspects of rest is its flexibility. It doesn't have to look a certain way or take a specific amount of time. It's not about lying in bed for 12 hours a day (though wouldn't that be nice, sometimes?).

Maybe, for you, rest is found in the quiet moments with a cup of tea and a good book. Perhaps it's found in the flow of an exercise sequence or the rhythm of your breath during a meditation session. For others, it could be a rejuvenating jog through a forest trail. The key is to find what rest looks like for you, and embrace it wholeheartedly.

So, while rest might be seen as an interlude to a busy life, its clear benefits position it as a pivotal point in life. It's about nurturing your body, nourishing your mind, and revitalising your spirit. In this light, rest isn't merely a suggestion—it becomes a beautiful necessity.

Rest is not a luxury; it's a vital ingredient for a more fulfilled, happier, and stress-free life. By incorporating rest into our daily routines, we can optimise our mental, physical, and emotional well-being. Rest enhances cognitive performance, improves physical health, boosts emotional resilience, and increases productivity.

Getting enough rest helps to nourish our minds and bodies, and unlock the true potential of a well-rested life. Rest is like a secret tool that equips you for success, helps you gain balance and promotes positive well-being. It can be restorative and healing, and makes the difference between giving up and achieving. So, the next time you think things are becoming just too much, don't give up immediately; have a rest, and notice how you feel afterwards.

> *Rest is the recipe of champions;*
> *you could say it's the secret sauce!*

Remember, my friend, there's no guilt in rest. We live in a world that equates busyness with success, where 'burnout' is worn almost like a badge of honour. It's now time to flip the script. In our pursuit of achieving more, let's not forget the power of resting more. We owe it to ourselves to balance the scales; to embrace the quiet moments, the soft pillows, the deep breaths, the closed eyes.

Here's your 'permission slip' to rest and recharge. Believe me, in using this, you'll be not only doing yourself a favour, but doing the world a favour, too.

I give myself permission to rest

Signed ....

(Insert your name)

9

FLOW

~

Being in flow is, to me, being more in 'soft' time where everything is going smoothly in my day. It could be waking just before the alarm has gone off, waltzing around the kitchen with a smile on my face as I get breakfast prepared, whilst the sun is shining which is always a bonus in England. I arrive early with plenty of time to ponder and, if I'm at a meeting, everything goes well, and people are left positively glowing with happiness. You know, the days where nothing could have gone any better.

This is in stark contrast to being out of flow or what I call being in 'hard' time. When nothing seems to be going according to plan, no matter how hard I try. You arrive late, transport is delayed or you're stuck in traffic. Perhaps you spill your coffee and have to wipe down your blazer or, worse, spill it on someone else! Or you arrive late for a conference and, even though you apologise profusely and say that this has never happened before, you're greeted with a glare that signifies that the other person doesn't completely believe you. Maybe this is because they have never met you before and, whether we like it or not, first impressions count—a little too much, in my opinion. Anyway, I'm sure you catch my drift.

Basically, when you are in flow, you feel much happier, more peaceful and content with what is going on right now. All is well in your world, and you need nothing more, for now anyway. This is just the right ingredient for your well-being because you are in perfect harmony with your body and mind and even the world seems to be a beautiful place; you couldn't possibly want to be else-where, as you are right where you need to be (Edwards, 1999).

Another way of looking at flow is by being in a *state* of flow. This is when you find yourself in a state of complete immersion and focus. It is often thought of as a complete game-changer, especially in the sphere of work. This state, referred to as 'flow', is often asso-ciated with a heightened sense of engage-ment and deep concentration, where time seems to fade away.

There are many transformative benefits of being in flow, which will be looked at shortly, along with ways to create new habits so that we can tap into this flow state more regularly. But before we explore this, let's first look at what flow is.

In essence, flow is a psychological state of optimal experience (Csikszentmihalyi, 1989). It is the sweet spot between the level of chal-lenge presented by a task and our personal skill level, resulting in a harmonious merging of action and awareness. When we are in flow, we become fully absorbed in the present moment, effortlessly executing tasks with heightened focus, creativity, and a deep sense of satisfaction.

Flow not only brings immense joy and fulfilment, but can also enhance our performance and overall well-being.

Here are some benefits of being in flow:

Enhancing Performance

When in flow, our cognitive abilities are optimised, and our performance reaches its peak. We experience heightened focus, clarity, and efficiency, leading to improved productivity and quality of work.

Deepening Learning

Flow promotes accelerated learning and skill acquisition. In this state, we are more receptive to new information, and our brain is primed for absorbing knowledge and making connections. Flow helps us engage in deliberate practice and master complex tasks more effectively.

Increasing Well-being

Flow provides a sense of intrinsic motivation, fulfilment, and joy. Immersed in activities we genuinely enjoy, we experience a sense of purpose, accomplishment, and positive emotions. The sustained engagement of flow can counteract stress, anxiety, and negative thoughts, leading to enhanced overall well-being.

Heightening Creativity

Flow unleashes our creative potential. As we enter a state of deep concentration and enter a flow state, our minds become attuned to novel ideas and insights. This heightened creativity extends beyond the task at hand, spilling over into other aspects of our lives.

As there are so many benefits, it's easy to understand the reason why it would be wonderful to get into this state of flow more regularly, perhaps even on a daily basis. As with anything in life, this doesn't come easily; but the more we can practice getting into this state of awareness, the more often it will come about, thus making our lives a little easier.

Here are some practical strategies to help cultivate these habits and facilitate entering the state of flow:

Identifying Flow-Inducing Activities

Take note of activities that consistently capture your attention and bring you joy. These can be hobbies, professional tasks, or creative pursuits. Identify the common elements that make these activities conducive to flow, such as a balance between challenge and skill level or a sense of autonomy.

Setting Clear Goals

Clearly define your goals and objectives for each activity. Well-defined goals provide a sense of direction and focus, allowing you to immerse yourself more fully in the task at hand.

Eliminating Distractions

Create an environment that minimises distractions. Turn off notifications on your phone, find a quiet space, and allocate dedicated time for your flow-inducing activities. This intentional space helps you concentrate and minimise external interruptions. A calm atmosphere invites quality and creative a chance to flourish, which is essential for producing high quality and productive work.

Cultivating Deep Work Routines

Establish routines that signal your brain to enter a state of deep focus. These can include setting aside specific time blocks, engaging in a brief meditation or breathing exercise, or listening to instrumental music that enhances concentration. I like to use an old-fashioned hourglass timer and then turn it upside down when the task is complete. At other times I use The Pomodoro Technique, which I mentioned in Chapter 8, whereby you work for 25 minutes and then take a 5 to 10-minute break, and continue this process for three tasks then take a longer, 30-minute break. This is quite a popular method used by many successful people.

Seeking Challenging Tasks

Continually seek out tasks that push the boundaries of your skill level. Flow emerges when challenges match or slightly exceed our abilities, so embrace opportunities for growth and skill development. This will also increase your motivation and enable you to keep the momentum.

Flow is a powerful and rewarding state that holds immense potential. It can enhance our daily lives at a deeper level. By intentionally cultivating habits that invite flow, we can experience heightened focus, improved performance, increased creativity, and overall well-being.

You don't have to try hard to be in a state of flow, that's part of the beauty of it. Just let go of the need to control everything, work with it and allow the state of flow to step in, bring ease into your everyday; you'll feel much better for doing so.

10

PEACE OF MIND

~

P eace is something many crave for but
for one reason or another, few allow
themselves the pleasure it brings. A little
peace and quiet can do immense good if we
allow ourselves the joy of it. Yet, why are so
many so afraid of it?

Perhaps it's being afraid of silence, with
nothing but your breath and the sound of
your beating heart to keep you company. I
know a couple of people who couldn't think
of anything worse than being quiet. But
peace in itself is something pure and this

sacred time gives us a gift. The gift of peace is something to be treasured. A miracle in itself.

For me peace of mind is a personal haven, a sanctuary where I can retreat, recover, and replenish. A place where I am free to be me. Somewhere I can close the door to the hustle and bustle and the noise that can all too often drown out my innermost thoughts. When I have peace, I have space to truly be and for me this is priceless.

Although finding solace and tranquility seems increasingly elusive. The significance of peace of mind cannot be overstated. It's the cornerstone of a fulfilling and balanced existence, providing numerous benefits that can permeate all aspects of our lives.

Peace can bring transformation in many ways; mentally, physically and emotionally, helping us to cultivate a happier, healthier, and stress-free life.

First, let's explore what having peace of mind means.

Peace of mind is a state of inner calmness, contentment, and harmony. It involves freeing oneself from worries, anxieties, and internal conflicts, allowing space for mental clarity, emotional stability, and overall well-being. It's an active choice to cultivate a sense of tranquility amidst life's challenges and uncertainties.

It isn't always easy to achieve inner peace, especially in times of chaos and drama, which unfortunately happens far too frequently in our modern world. But by attempting to create this, it will enable you to remain calm in a crisis, helping you to make clearer and more rational decisions. This is an increasing necessity, especially in a busy and crowded environment. Peace of mind is indeed a gift that when practiced can be extremely rewarding.

Here are some benefits to having peace of mind:

Enhancing Mental Well-being

Peace of mind has positive impact on mental well-being, acting like a shield from anxiety, depression and stressors from everyday life. While not being completely preventative, it can certainly help. When you are at peace you're better able to cope with challenges and can think more clearly and better able to be solution orientated. As opposed to feeling overwhelmed.

Improving Physical Health

The mind and body are intricately connected, and peace of mind plays a pivotal role in maintaining physical well-being. Moreover, achieving peace of mind can help improve sleep quality. I know far too well from tossing and turning at night, desperate to get to sleep but worrying about something I said or not said, something I did or didn't do, especially when I was working for an impatient boss. You might be familiar with this.

Finding peace can help you let go of what you can't do and feel more at ease. I find telling myself that 'there's nothing you can do at this present moment, so not sleeping or lying awake thinking about won't make any difference whatsoever Pamela, so you may as well sleep'.

This usually works and before I know it I'm off to la-la land. I also find that the more I try to stay awake, guess what? The more I find myself drifting off. Peace of mind can also enhance the body's immune system, thus, keeping our body functioning optimally, and that always feels great!

Greater Emotional Resilience

Peace of mind fortifies emotional resilience by enabling you to navigate life's challenges with grace and composure. When inner peace is cultivated, emotional reactivity diminishes, allowing for healthier responses to stress, conflicts, and setbacks. A greater level of peace of mind can help you react calmly and thoughtfully, strengthening our relationships with others. Thus, leading to greater overall life satisfaction and fulfilment.

Better Relationships

We tend to lash out or withdraw when we're stressed or anxious. It's not easy I know, especially if you're having a disagreement with your loved one about who said what and when. But taking a step back can help you gather your thoughts, take a breath, look at the bigger picture and allow yourself to get all warm and fuzzy again and step back into the conversation. Only this time, you're coming from a place of love and peace, which feels heaps better.

Increasing Happiness and Reducing Stress

Peace of mind provides a foundation for happiness and a stress-free life. When we detach ourselves from the incessant noise of worries and anxieties, we create space for joy, gratitude, and contentment to flourish. Peace of mind equips us with the ability to remain centred amidst life's challenges and embrace a more positive outlook.

Boosting Productivity

When you're at peace, you focus better. Your mind isn't cluttered with worries and what-ifs. You are capable of accomplishing more, faster and with better quality.

There are countless reasons why these would enhance your life but unless you incorporate them into your daily life, they will remain just 'a nice to have', as opposed to something you can apply and help to maintain a truly fulfilled and happier life. Fitting these practices into your daily life is the first hurdle to overcome. But don't let this put you off.

Here are some ways to include cultivating peace as part of your everyday life:

Intentional Practices

Engage intentional practices, such as meditation and deep breathing exercises, allows you to cultivate a present-moment awareness and detach from anxious thoughts. Breathing is to the mind what a cooling system is to a computer. It helps prevent overheating. By focusing on our breath, we can anchor ourselves in the present moment and break free from our tangled thoughts.

Allocating even just a few minutes each day to such practices can significantly contribute to a greater sense of peace and mental clarity. I try and do this daily and if for some reason I skip it or forget to do it I really notice the difference. If I miss it I find myself getting irritable and I admit a tad grouchy, especially if I have a deadline or a meeting to get to and I'm running late.

But, when I do my meditation practice, I seem to glide through the day, taking each task as it comes, and everything seems to just run much smoother and flow. Life is a breeze. And, even if there are challenges, I think because I feel calmer, I'm not thrown off guard and find it easier to manage. Try it for yourself and notice how you feel and the difference it makes.

It's also worthwhile doing a reflection exercise in the evening and seeing what has worked and what hasn't gone quite as well as you have hoped. If this is the case, please don't beat yourself up! Simply try and work out what you could have done differently, adjust your stance and perhaps the things you do and the way you do them accordingly. Remember, nothing is set in stone. It's definitely a test and try method. Do what works for you. You will get there.

Setting Boundaries

Establishing healthy boundaries in personal and professional relationships helps protect our peace of mind. Reduce the time spent with negative people or on social media platforms that breed comparison and discontent.

Learning to say no when necessary, prioritising self-care, and creating space for solitude and reflection are essential steps in nurturing our inner tranquility.

This, however, is sometimes easier said than done, especially if you have a tendency to people-please. I find thinking of it as practice helps. For instance, the next time someone invites you for lunch and you really don't want to go but you feel obligated to. Practice saying 'no'. Try it on for size, like you would a jacket and see how it fits. At first it may feel a little uncomfortable but the more often you get into it, the more comfortable it'll feel and soon it'll come naturally, and you'll wear it with ease. Although, the other person may not like it at first, they will probably respect you for having the courage to say a polite no thank you.

Practicing Forgiveness

Holding onto grudges is like carrying a heavy backpack during a marathon. It hinders our progress and saps our energy. Forgiving doesn't mean forgetting or accepting harmful actions; it means freeing ourselves from the burden of resentment and bitterness, Instead choose to forgive and focus on creating a positive and peaceful mind.

Embracing Acceptance

Acceptance of the present moment, embracing imperfections, and letting go of control over things beyond our influence are crucial aspects of cultivating peace of mind. It involves shifting our focus from dwelling on past regrets or worrying about an uncertain future to fully experiencing and appreciating the present. Let's embrace imperfections, instead of obsessing over every mistake, which never works and makes you feeling less than. Instead just let it go and notice how much lighter and freer you feel.

Being Grateful

Practicing gratitude changes our perspective and allows us to find peace in our existing circumstances. Doing this regularly helps you feel like you have enough and more importantly, that you are enough and that my friend, is a *big* deal.

In a nutshell, peace of mind is priceless it can transform our lives positively, benefiting our mental, physical, and emotional well-being. By consciously nurturing inner calmness, we unlock the door to a happier, healthier, and more fulfilling existence.

Make peace of mind a priority, and notice the difference it can make to your life.

11

MINDFULNESS

~

Mindfulness is a hot topic. Something that many want to achieve but only a few do, or at least that's how it's portrayed for the average person. I mean, if the real world is anything to go by, who actually has time for mindfulness anyway?

Contrary to popular belief, however, being mindful doesn't necessarily take up more time. It could be woven into your everyday routines, to give you a sense of peace and inner focus whenever you most need it.

The truth is, we could all do with a little bit more mindfulness in our lives, if only to rescue us from the maddening mess of distractions we have become so familiar with. From incessant notifications, to emails dropping into your inbox. From sudden alerts and apparently 'urgent' messages from people who say the all too often 'expiring soon', to other 'Don't miss out' FOMO (Fear of missing out) prompts, suggesting you'll be missing out on the latest craze, trend, offer etc. You catch my drift?

Yes, mindfulness is very-much needed. Personally, I think this brings a sense of relief; if we can practice it more often, we can then add a sense of calm to the utter chaos that has crept into our standard routines. "But how on earth can we do this effectively, Pamela?", I hear you say. Well, I have a few ideas that I think may help. Try them out; at worst you'll have more stories to share with others about your tales of trying mindfulness for yourself. At best, you'll have added tools for your well-being and self-care toolkit, and you never know when the moment will arise when you'll need to reach for it. So, without further ado, let's further explore this wonderful world of mindfulness.

Understanding Mindfulness

First, let's describe what this is. Mindfulness, rooted in ancient, contemplative traditions, is the art of bringing one's attention to the present moment with non-judgmental awareness. It involves focusing intentionally on sensations, thoughts, and emotions occurring in the present, without getting caught up in any past regrets or future worries. By cultivating mindfulness, we can train our minds to be fully present, and accepting of the current experience.

Why is Mindfulness Good for Us?

This is a timeless practice that's been gaining widespread recognition for its profound benefits. By developing the habit of mindfulness, incorporating it into our daily lives, we can enhance our overall well-being, reduce any stress, and cultivate a greater sense of balance.

Enhancing Well-being and Reducing Stress

Mindfulness has a positive impact on mental and physical health. Evidence shows that mindfulness meditation significantly reduced symptoms of anxiety and depression in participants. A study consisting of an eight-week program with mindful meditation, conducted by researchers at Harvard Medical School, demonstrated that mindfulness practice led to changes in brain regions associated with self-awareness, compassion, stress and memory (McGreevey, 2011).

Incorporating mindfulness into a daily routine can serve as a powerful tool for managing stress and promoting overall well-being.

Here are some ways we can develop mindful habits to achieve this:

(please read the following instructions first, as they involve closed eyes).

Begin with breathing

Allocate a few minutes each day to focus on your breath. Close your eyes gently, then take slow, deep breaths; observe the sensations of each breath entering and leaving your body. This simple practice can anchor you in the present moment and cultivate a sense of calm.

Engage in mindful eating

Before your next meal, take a moment to appreciate the colours, textures, and smells of the food in front of you. Slowly savour each bite, paying attention to flavours and sensations. This practice encourages mindful eating, bringing a deeper connection with your food, and enhancing the overall dining experience.

Embrace mindfulness in daily activities

Incorporate mindfulness into your daily routine by choosing one activity to do with heightened awareness. It could be brushing your teeth, taking a shower, or walking. Engage your senses, notice the details, and

let go of distractions. By infusing mindfulness into routine tasks, you can transform
those tasks into opportunities for self-reflec-
tion and presence.

You can bring greater calm into your current
situation by taking your time with activities,
doing things a little slower. You may like to
do something creative, like painting, drawing
or playing an instrument. You may prefer
gardening, creating a lovely meal, or simply
sitting down and stroking your cat or dog, if
you have one. Doing an activity you love can
instantly calm your nervous system and help
you enjoy life more as you immerse yourself
in the wonderful, present moment.

Practice gratitude

Take a few moments each day to reflect on
the things you're grateful for. Whether that's
a beautiful sunset, a kind gesture from a
friend, or a personal achievement; cultivating
gratitude can shift your focus towards the
positive aspects of life, and foster a deeper
sense of contentment.

Balance and Well-being

Granted, this all takes time, patience and practice, but, by consistently incorporating mindfulness practices into our lives, we can achieve a more balanced and fulfilling existence.

Mindfulness helps us become more aware of our thoughts and emotions, allowing us to respond to life's challenges with clarity and equanimity. It encourages us to cultivate self-compassion, enabling us to better navigate stress, adversity, and self-criticism.

Moreover, mindfulness practices can improve cognitive functions, such as attention, memory, and creativity. By training our minds to be more focused and present, we can enhance our productivity and overall performance in various areas of life.

As you can see, mindfulness doesn't have to be just a passing trend; instead, it offers potential as a transformative practice that can stand the test of time. Its benefits extend far beyond momentary relaxation, empowering individuals to lead more balanced, joyful, and meaningful lives. By developing mindful habits, we can tap into the profound benefits of reducing stress, enhancing well-being, and, ultimately, cultivating a harmonious relationship with ourselves and the world around us.

12

BE PRESENT

~

With constant tugs at our attention from a relentless stream of notifications and to-do lists, it's no wonder that the art of being present—truly engaging with the here and now—can seem almost lost. We tend to race from one obligation to the next, our minds buzzing with plans, reflections, and reactions. But what if the secret to a fuller, more satisfying life isn't in the endless pursuit of future goals, but instead, in keeping on choosing to savour the present moment?

Think about this for a moment. Have you ever gone for a walk, without any particular purpose or agenda? Such as taking a stroll through the forest. Ask yourself the following questions to help you absorb this moment:

- What can you see?
- What can you hear?
- What can you smell?

I often like to do this. I find that exploring different scenery transports me away from any daily troubles or tribulations I may have going on. While I'm out and about, I walk like I don't have a care in the world; as though, at this point in time, nothing else matters—especially any problems. Perhaps you can relate?

Funnily enough, after I return from my stroll, the problem that has been taking up unnecessary headspace suddenly doesn't seem so big at all. It's all perspective I guess. A change of scenery can often help in this way. I continue to find that, if I've been trying to find a solution about something, then stepping away, if only for a moment or two, can make all the difference. There's been many an occasion when I've departed with a question and returned with an answer, or at least a different outlook.

Being present and connecting with your surroundings or people around you, even in a small way, can make all the difference to your overall well-being. There are many reasons for this, which I'll now expand on.

Why Being Present is a Game-Changer

First, let's talk about the reason that being present (or mindful), isn't just about focusing on trendy buzzwords. It involves a practice that's been endorsed by psychological research and philosophical wisdom alike, for its profound benefits.

Here's what tuning into the present moment can offer you:

Less Stress

When you focus on the now, the cacophony of worries about the future and the past fades away, leaving a quiet space that allows your mind to rest. This mental break can significantly lower your stress levels.

Deeper Connection

Being present means actively listening and engaging with others, which enables deeper connections and understanding. Your conversations become more meaningful, building stronger, more authentic relationships.

Greater Enjoyment

Have you ever noticed how much more vivid everything seems when you really pay attention? Food tastes richer, music resonates more deeply, and everyday pleasures become more enjoyable. Being present amplifies your experiences.

Improved Health

This might seem far-fetched, but it's true. Lower stress levels contribute to better overall health. Studies have shown that mindfulness practices can lower blood pressure (Carlson et al., 2007), and even enhance immune function (Ngô, 2013).

Simple Ways to Be More Present

This focus sounds great, right? But how do you start embracing the present, when your brain is used to juggling a million things?

Don't worry! There are many practices to help you ease into a more present lifestyle, which we will explore next.

Breathing with Intention

This is something we do automatically, and rarely think about it. Try focusing on your breathing now—take a deep, slow inhale, followed by a gradual exhale. Notice how the air feels as it moves within you; focus on that sensation. This simple act can centre you in the present moment.

Indulging in the Details

Pick a routine activity, like having your morning coffee or another drink. Use your senses to help you focus on every aspect of it. For instance, notice the warmth of the cup in your hands, smell the aroma, see the patterns in the coffee's surface, and notice the taste as you take a sip. Engaging your senses is a powerful way to anchor yourself in the 'now'.

Device Detox

Our devices are attention-grabbers. Try setting aside specific times in your day for using them, or allocate locations in your home where phones, tablets, and laptops are off-limits. It might feel odd at first, but this break from constant connectivity can free you up, so you can engage with the immediate world around you.

I have a friend who applies this rule and extends it to anyone entering her home. Whenever she has visitors, she asks them to place their mobile in a basket before they enter the living room; she explains that she wants to give them her undivided attention and spend quality time with them. After any awkward, uncomfortable moments have passed, where the visitors 'settle in' to this idea, the fun begins and nobody mentions it again—until it's time to leave, when they collect their devices.

That practice may sound harsh, but she finds it works well for her. You can make up your own rules and routines, of course. But if you like this idea, once you get into the new way of doing things, I'm sure you'll notice the difference—as will your friends and family.

Active Listening

When you're in conversation, make an effort to listen and really hear the other person. This means not just waiting for your turn to speak, but engaging fully with what they're saying. You'll be surprised at the nuances and emotions you can pick up on.

Moving Mindfully

Whether it's walking, or even just stretching at your desk, deliberate, intentional movement can be incredibly rewarding. Notice how your body feels with each motion, observing things like its capability and strength.

Gratitude Reminders

There are times when the present moment doesn't feel that great. For those times, having a mental (or physical) list of things you're grateful for can help to anchor you in the present.

I like to set reminders on my smartphone or another device, about what I'm grateful for. You could also set reminders on any smart speakers at home. These can give you an instant pick-me-up and may make you smile as you carry on with your day.

Becoming more present isn't a goal you reach; it's a continual process. Some days it'll feel natural, and on others, it may feel like a struggle. That's okay. The key isn't to achieve an ideal state of eternal mindfulness, but to keep bringing your focus back to where life is happening. Be here now; be fully present, right here, right now.

The journey to being present is your own, and every moment you fully engage with can add richness to your life. So, next time your mind starts to wander to the 'what if' and 'if only' thoughts, remember that your power lies in the now. Embrace it, engage with it, and watch how it transforms your life.

CONCLUSION

~

Now that you've had a chance to explore the beauty of slowing down and savouring each moment as it unfolds, and even as the world continues to embrace busyness and productivity as the 'norm', I hope you realise that your worth doesn't have to be measured by the number of tasks crossed off your to-do list. It can be assessed instead through the depth of connections you build—with yourself and those around you.

You've discovered that the power of presence isn't just a luxury, reserved for retreats and special occasions; it's a necessity and can be captured even in the busiest times, amidst everyday chaos. It's not about adding more to your plate, instead, it's savouring what's already on it. Neither is it about finding extra hours in your day but, rather, making the most of the time you do have. This may involve, replacing an existing task, that no longer serves you, to something you find more fulfilling.

It is possible to find respite from the relentless pace of life, to reconnect with your inner self, and to rediscover the joy of staying present.

Remember, this journey is not about perfection; it's about progress. Yes, there will still be days when life feels overwhelming, when the urge to rush creeps in—and that's okay. The key is to acknowledge those moments without judgment, and gently guide yourself back to the present.

Our challenge is not to control and try to do everything, but to let go of the outcome—without fear—and observe what happens.

Treat it a little like an experiment, with you playing the role of the observer, questioning with curiosity; will the world fall apart? What would happen if you chose to simply just 'be'? Notice what happens when you try this approach, and track any changes, to help manage your thoughts and feelings going forward.

I suggest, taking the time, if only for a short while, to find the beauty in a moment as you explore the great adventure that allows you to just be. This will help nourish and increase levels of fulfilment more than you can imagine. Enjoy the experience as you embrace the miracle of each unfolding moment.

The great thing about this is that by unlocking the treasure trove of tools you now have, you get to explore your deepest, most heartfelt potential and live a more fulfilled life. The very best part is that you get to have all of this and more, just by being *you*.

You now get to come home to you. The *real*

you, the version nobody else has seen—that is, until this moment.

Now it's your turn to be the person you're meant to be.

Because, if not now, then when?

Don't get so busy making plans for the future that you forget to live now.

Life isn't something you wait for, that's way ahead in the future.

Instead, make sure you're ready to be here now.

You can never get this moment back again, so savour it, because now is where the party's at!

Now is the place of power, the turning point. It could be a chance to hit refresh on your life—or press pause if you prefer.

You get to choose and decide.

Your time is now.

So, what are you going to do?

As for me, well I don't know what's in store for tomorrow. But, for now, I'm going to stay a while and play...happy being part of life's adventure.

As you prepare to finish this book, I invite you to try this little exercise (please read the instructions first as it involves closed eyes) So, close your eyes for a moment. Now breathe. Feel the air filling your lungs; feel the ground beneath your feet, and the rhythm of your heart. This moment is yours —it's a sanctuary of peace that you can return to at any time you want.

Carry this presence with you, as you step back into the stream of life. Remember, you are capable and deserving of every drop of joy that life has to offer. By staying present, you're not just surviving the whirlwind of life; you're thriving in it. You're not just doing; you're being—beautifully being.

Thank you for letting me be a part of your journey.

Keep in mind that this is just the beginning. There are more journeys, more insights, more moments of joy awaiting. So create your very own safe haven from stress and unwarranted distraction. Enjoy your oasis of calm, where you flourish as you slow down. Stay present and just 'be', for as long as you wish...

SHARE THE LOVE

I hope you have enjoyed reading this book,
as much as I have enjoyed writing it.
If you have, it will mean the world to me,
if you would kindly leave a review
and share your experience with a friend.

Want to stay in touch?
Join my Author Friends Email List, and
receive your Free digital gift, at:
pamelasommers.com

ACKNOWLEDGMENTS

I thank God for blessing me.
I'd like to thank you, reader,
for taking the time to read my book.
I wish you a life full of calm and deep joy
in the present moment.
May love, peace and happiness be yours.

For my editor, Diana McMahon Collis
I want you to know that
I truly appreciate your
continued support and encouragement.
You are a Godsend.

THANK YOU

REFERENCES

Carlson, Linda E. et al, 'One year pre–post intervention follow-up of psychological, immune, endocrine and blood pressure outcomes of mindfulness-based stress reduction (MBSR) in breast and prostate cancer outpatients', *Brain, Behavior, and Immunity* [online journal], 21(8) (November 2007), pp. 1038-1049. <https://doi.org/10.1016/j.bbi.2007.04.002> accessed 28 February 2024.

Cirillo, F. *The Pomodoro Technique*. United Kingdom: Virgin Books.

Csikszentmihalyi, M *Flow: The Psychology of Optimal Experience*. United States: Harper and Row.

Edwards, G. *Pure Bliss: The Art of Living in Soft Time*. United Kingdom: Piatkus.

McGreevey, S. 'Eight weeks to a better brain', *The Harvard Gazette* [website], *(*21 January 2011). <https://news.harvard.edu/gazette/story/2011/01/eight-weeks-to-a-better-brain/> accessed 28 February 2024.

Ngô, T.L. 'Review of the effects of mindfulness meditation on mental and physical health and its mechanisms of action', *Santé Mentale au Québec* [online journal], 38(2) (2013), 19-34. <https://doi.org/10.7202/1023988ar> accessed 28 February 2024.

Stulberg, B. & Magness, S. *Peak Performance: Elevate Your Game, Avoid Burnout, and Thrive with the New Science of Success*. United States : Rodale Books.

ABOUT THE AUTHOR

Pamela Sommers is the author of the following titles:

- *Life lessons from a 40 Something... : For the Best Start in Life*
- *Building Castles In The Sky: How to Make Your Dreams Come True*
- *Fabulously You Series*

  - Book One: Fabulously You: Live a Life You Love

- Book Two: Fabulously You: Feel Amazing & Thrive

Pamela has been featured in a number of publications including *Success* magazine,

The Independent, Metro, Belfast Telegraph, House of Coco and *Spotlight* magazines, as well as the *HuffPost, Thrive Global* and *LadyBoss-Blogger* blogs, with her tips and advice.

She is the founder of *SommerSparkle*, an award-winning online boutique that provides beautiful jewellery and accessories, which have been showcased in a number of magazines including *British Vogue*.

Pamela is passionate about inspiring others to make their dreams come true.

She loves to dance, listen to music, and enjoys painting. She currently lives in the suburbs of London, England with her family.

You can find her online via her website: pamelasommers.com

Instagram: @pamela.sommers

READ MORE FROM THE
AUTHOR...

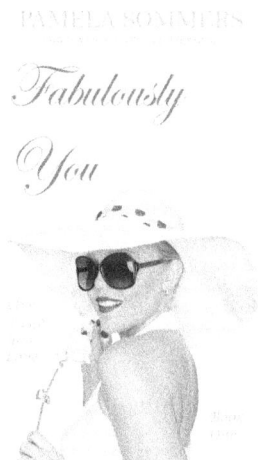

Fabulously You:
Live a Life You Love
(Book One)

Pamela's bestselling, personal growth book helps you to reconnect and re-discover yourself. It empowers you to live a life that's true to you.

Here's what people are saying about it:

'For those who are fearful of the future, this is one to read.'

'I also liked the author's emphasis on looking after yourself, bringing love, kindness and tenderness back into our lives and, most importantly, being true to ourselves.'

'A toolkit for life filled with happy delights.'

'Ms. Sommers hits the nail right on the head with her life observations and positive advice. Each chapter is devoted to a specific "life lesson" that offers encouragement and inspiration to be the very best version of yourself you can be. I recommend this book for anyone interested in a positive attitude adjustment or anyone looking for ways to change their outlook on life.'

'Sunshine in a book, a go-to for happy living.'

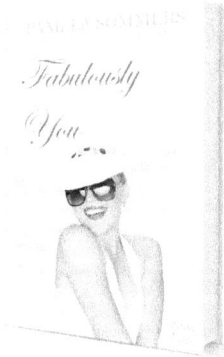

Fabulously You: Feel Amazing & Thrive
(Book Two)

Pamela's bestselling, personal growth book helps you to reignite your passion and be the hero of your life. It motivates you to be your best and live a life you're excited about.

Here's what people are saying about it:

'A feel-good book that motivates and encourages the reader to take on anything in life! A boost of sunshine guaranteed to give extra smiles and enlightenment!'

'I highly recommend this book and will be spreading the word to my girlfriends who need a good little pep talk on self-love and self-care. Excellently put together.'

'Powerful and inspiring, this book is a journey back to yourself. A reminder of your inherent spark. The fire that burns within. '

'I am so glad that I came across it. This isn't your ordinary self-help book... As someone who has struggled to see her self-worth, it was wonderful to read something that could get me on the right path to love myself again, to feel that I am worthy after dedicating my life to my family.'

'I recommend this as a good feeling read to help inject a little optimism into their mindset! Nicely done.'

Life Lessons from a 40 something...:
For The Best Start In Life

Pamela's award-winning, bestselling, self-improvement book is filled with big-hearted advice, to empower and inspire you to go for your dreams—regardless of your current circumstances. It is based on her own life.

Here's what people are saying about it:

'An easy read and truly inspirational, even life changing.'

'This book imparts lessons, with each chapter
delivering its own lesson theme, such as, "Don't
compare yourself to others," etc. Some include
how the author came to learn these lessons, and
most include why they are important.'

'As a therapist, these are all the same lessons that
I strive to teach my clients so that they may live
healthy lives that are true to their values and
selves. There is great wisdom in this book, and I
wish I had read it when I was about fifteen. You
will be glad you picked it up, and hopefully you
will share it, too.'

'Sound advice written in an informal manner
from a personal perspective. There are things in
this book that just reading the words alone will
have a massive impact on a person. Realising
you in yourself are enough can go a long way.
For me, this book is about trusting who you are,
even if you're not quite sure who that is. After all,
you always change and grow... Easily accessible,
not preachy, and very insightful.'

'Big-hearted advice from a wise lady. This is a
warm and useful book that I would recommend

to anyone from the age of 16 to 40. It covers all the issues that make someone a happy, thriving, successful member of society—from love relationships to being confident in the workplace to how to look great. The author writes clearly in a style that can be understood and applied by any age group, and she gives examples of exercises you can use to implement the ideas she suggests...
The new material you do take away will help you live a happier, more fulfilled life.'

'Life Lessons is a book that I wish I would have read years ago. It gives you much-needed wisdom to conquer all the obstacles that you will experience in life, as well as giving you sound advice for getting through the highs and lows. This is a book that should be read by teenagers and twentysomethings, to avoid any quarter-life crisis. As I knock on the door of 40, these are lessons that I still can apply.'

'Although geared toward teenagers and young adults, "Life Lessons from a 40 something" has all sorts of good advice applicable for all ages,

even those of us who are fortysomething, as well.
A pleasant read, full of Ms. Sommers' personal
experiences and the lessons she learned over the
years.'— The International Review of Books

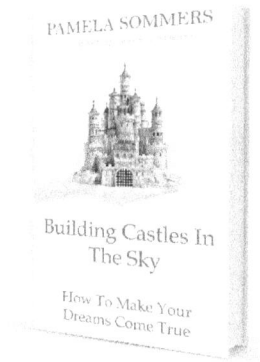

Building Castles In The Sky: How To Make Your Dreams Come True

Pamela's bestselling, personal growth book is filled with spiritual secrets for success, to help make your dreams come true.

Here's what people are saying about it:

'An uplifting and helpful book, for all those wishing to become the best version of themselves.'

'I really enjoyed reading this positive and uplifting self-help book. I plan to put her suggestions into practice. I am looking forward to positive change.'

'This book is easy to follow and understand. I recommend it to anyone looking to improve their life. It is confidence-inspiring for any age reader.

I commend the author for sharing these valuable insights into life and how to make it better.'

'Wonderful - It's an inspiring guide to those seeking calm and peace in a chaotic world. I read it as part of my therapy for social anxiety, and I will definitely be recommending it to others.'

'There are some excellent examples of behaviour (I found myself in there a number of times) and a heap of advice and tips on how to changes your thoughts and get back on track. An easy read, highly recommended.'

'If only I had read her book earlier, because my ride would definitely have been smoother and easier with her help!'

'The author's references to Biblical times and scriptures from the Bible bring relevance to Christians. "God wants us to experience all the good things in life." The author shares personal stories of her journey and a roadmap with tools for 'building castles in the sky', guiding you through the steps you will need to take, in an easy-to- understand writing style.'

Available at leading book retailers.

www.ingramcontent.com/pod-product-compliance
Lightning Source LLC
La Vergne TN
LVHW052026080426
835513LV00018B/2182